Fact Finders®

THE INVENTION OF THE AIRPLANE

by Lucy Beevor

CAPSTONE PRESS
a capstone imprint

Fact Finders Books are published by Capstone Press,
1710 Roe Crest Drive, North Mankato, Minnesota 56003
www.mycapstone.com

Library of Congress Cataloging-in-Publication Data
Name: Beevor, Lucy, author.
Title: The Invention of the Airplane/by Lucy Beevor.
Other titles: Airplane
Description: North Mankato, Minnesota: Capstone Press, 2018
Series: Fact Finders. World-Changing Inventions. | Age: 8–10.
Includes bibliographical references and index.
Identifiers: LCCN 2017039183 (print) | LCCN 2017044048 (ebook)
ISBN 9781515798415 (library binding)
ISBN 9781515798491 (paperback)
ISBN 9781515798576 (eBook PDF)
Subjects: LCSH: Airplanes—History—Juvenile literature.
Classification: LCC TL670.3 (ebook) | LCC TL670.3 .S543 2018 (print)
DDC 629.133/34—dc23
LC record available at https://lccn.loc.gov/2017039183

Editorial Credits
Jennifer Huston, editor; Heidi Thompson, designer; Eric Gohl, media researcher; Katy LaVigne, production specialist

Original Edition Author
Julie L. Sinclair

Photo Credits
Alamy: ClassicStock, 7, Niday Picture Library, 6; Getty Images: Underwood Archives, 21; Granger, NYC: 12; Library of Congress: 15; Newscom: akg-images, 13, Everett Collection, 20, Picture History, 4 (all), UIG Universal Images Group/Underwood Archives, 23; Shutterstock: Carlos E. Santa Maria, 24, Chris Parypa Photography, 26, Ensuper, cover (middle), Everett Historical, 8, 9, fotoslaz, cover (top left & bottom), goodmoments, 17, Graham Bloomfield, 25, ifong, 2–3, 18–19, Michal Jurkowski, cover (top right), Nicku, 11, phive, cover (middle left), vectorEps, 22, Wojciech Beczynski, cover (middle right); Thinkstock: Claudio Divizia, 10

Design Elements: Shutterstock

Printed in the United States 5208

TABLE OF CONTENTS

Chapter 1: A Gift for Two Boys 4

Chapter 2: Before the Airplane 6

Chapter 3: Great Inventors 10

Chapter 4: How Airplanes Work 16

Chapter 5: The World Begins to Fly 20

Chapter 6: Airplanes Today 24

Timeline 29

Glossary 30

Critical Thinking Questions 31

Read More 31

Internet Sites 32

Index 32

1

A GIFT FOR TWO BOYS

One day in 1878, Milton Wright brought a gift home to his two youngest sons. Orville was 7 years old. Wilbur was 11. The gift was a toy helicopter made of cork, bamboo, paper, and a rubber band.

Orville (left) and Wilbur Wright grew up in the United States in the late 1800s. They dreamed of one day building and flying an airplane.

Milton showed the boys how to make the helicopter fly. He wound the two **propellers** and tossed the toy into the air. The boys were amazed when the helicopter flew. Eventually the helicopter broke, but it had sparked their imaginations. From that day forward, Wilbur and Orville wanted to build a flying machine. One day they hoped to ride in the machine and fly through the sky.

DID YOU KNOW?

Children played with toy helicopters for more than 100 years before full-sized **aircraft** were built.

propeller—a rotating blade that provides the force to move an aircraft through the air
aircraft—a vehicle that flies through the air

2 BEFORE THE AIRPLANE

Until the late 1800s, most people did not travel very far from their homes. They traveled by horse and wagon or they walked. For those who needed to travel long distances, it took weeks—sometimes months—to get to their **destinations**. But scientists and inventors were building new machines that would change travel forever.

Traveling by horse and wagon was slow and uncomfortable.

destination—the place where someone is traveling

NEW WAYS TO TRAVEL

Engines powered by steam, gasoline, and electricity led to the invention of trains and automobiles, which could travel longer distances. They were much faster than walking or traveling by horse and wagon. This made it easier for people to travel farther away from home.

Before automobiles and airplanes, many people traveled by train.

DID YOU KNOW?

The first train rail in the United States was laid in 1828. By 1900 more than 190,000 miles (305,700 kilometers) of tracks crossed the country.

Trains and automobiles did not fix all travel problems. Automobiles didn't always make traveling easy. Early automobiles were uncomfortable. They did not have springs to make the ride smooth. They also didn't have heaters. Early automobiles were unsafe and difficult to drive. Plus, there were very few road rules, which often led to accidents.

Early automobiles were not easy to drive and that sometimes led to accidents.

Trains had problems too. They could only travel where there were railroad tracks, so they didn't go everywhere people wanted to go. Trains also needed many people to care for the tracks. A train could run off its tracks if the tracks were damaged.

Trains were not always a safe way to travel. The Great Chatsworth Train Wreck occurred in Illinois in 1887. More than 80 people were killed.

People wanted to make traveling easier and safer. Some inventors made better engines for automobiles, but others began to think about a new way of traveling. They dreamed of flying in the air like birds.

3 GREAT INVENTORS

Before and after the inventions of the train and automobile, people tried to figure out how to build machines that would carry them safely through the air.

LEONARDO DA VINCI

Leonardo da Vinci was one of the first people to **design** a flying machine. Da Vinci lived in Italy in the late 1400s and early 1500s. He designed several machines with flapping wings that he called "ornithopters."

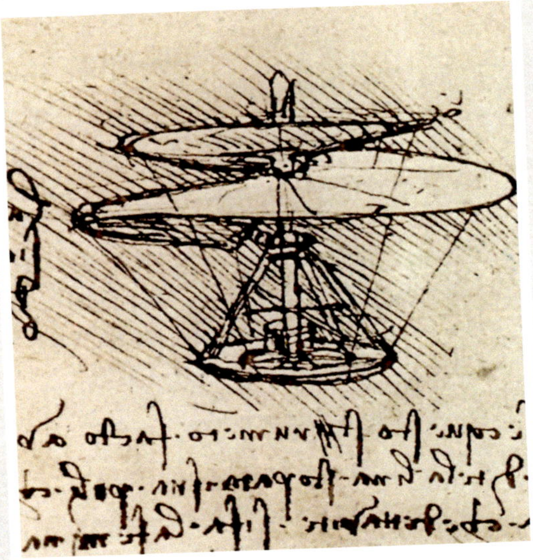

Leonardo da Vinci sketched a flying machine he called an airscrew. It is similar to a modern-day helicopter.

DID YOU KNOW?

Leonardo da Vinci designed many early machines. They included an armored car, a parachute, and another type of flying machine that looked like a helicopter.

THE MONTGOLFIER BROTHERS

In 1783 Joseph-Michel and Jacques-Étienne Montgolfier built a hot-air balloon. But the French brothers were not sure if it was safe for people to ride in. To find out, they put a sheep, a duck, and a rooster in the balloon's basket. These animals became the world's first hot-air balloon passengers. The animals landed safely after being in the air about eight minutes. In November of that year, the first human passengers took a 25-minute flight over Paris in the Montgolfier brothers' balloon.

The Montgolfier brothers tested their first hot-air balloon in 1783.

design—to create the shape or style of something

SIR GEORGE CAYLEY

In 1804 British **engineer** Sir George Cayley built a special model **glider**. With a movable tail and a kite-shaped wing set on a stick, it looked somewhat like a modern airplane. By 1853, Cayley had created the first full-sized glider. When he asked his assistant to fly the glider, the test was a success. It was the first glider flight to carry a passenger.

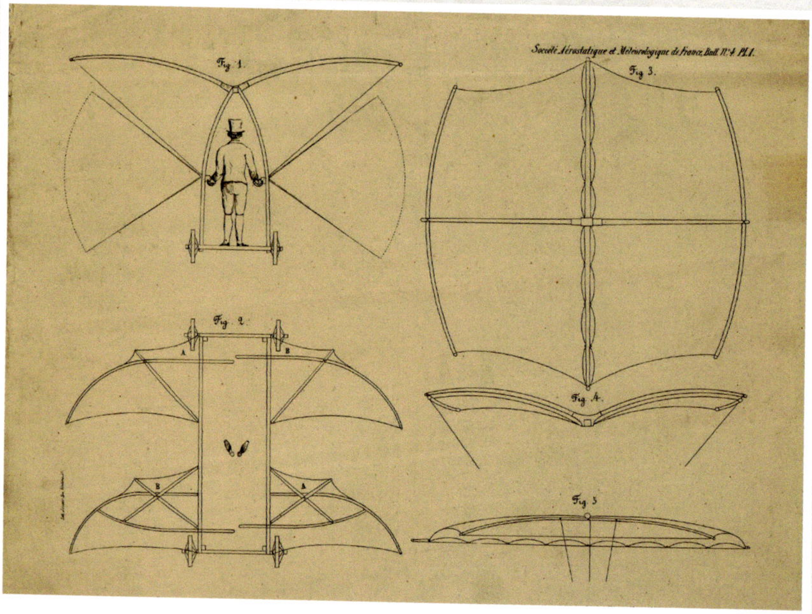

Sir George Cayley is sometimes called the father of **aviation**. This illustration shows his drawing of the glider.

engineer—someone trained to design and build machines, vehicles, bridges, roads, or other structures
glider—a lightweight aircraft that flies by floating and rising on air currents instead of by engine power
aviation—the science of building and flying aircraft

OTTO LILIENTHAL

German inventor Otto Lilienthal made his first flying machine in 1891. This hang glider had large wings and could soar through the air. Lilienthal later built many other successful gliders.

Otto Lilienthal made more than 2,000 flights in his hang gliders. Some of them reached more than 1,000 feet (305 meters) up in the air.

THE WRIGHT BROTHERS

Wilbur and Orville Wright studied flying and **mechanics** for many years. They tested models and built and flew large gliders and kites. But they wanted to build a flying machine that powered itself.

The brothers worked hard to make an airplane. They designed and built a lightweight engine and also made a propeller. Finally, in December 1903, their first airplane was ready. They called it the *Flyer.* It measured 21 feet (6.4 meters) long and its wings were 40.5 feet (12.3 m) wide. It weighed 605 pounds (274.4 kilograms) without a pilot.

mechanics—a part of science that deals with the way forces affect still or moving objects

TAKING TO THE SKIES

On December 17, 1903, the brothers took the *Flyer* to the sand dunes near Kitty Hawk, North Carolina. Orville sat in the pilot's seat, and Wilbur ran along the side. Their plane flew 120 feet (37 m) in 12 seconds. It was the first time that a self-powered machine had risen, flown in a straight line, and landed safely.

The Wright brothers flew the *Flyer* for the first time on December 17, 1903. It was only in the air for 12 seconds, but it made history.

4 HOW AIRPLANES WORK

The four forces of flight help people understand how airplanes fly. These forces are **thrust**, **lift**, weight, and **drag**.

THRUST AND LIFT

Thrust moves an airplane forward. A jet engine creates thrust and pushes the airplane forward. Most propeller engines also pull the plane forward. Thrust works with lift to make the airplane rise and fly.

Lift lets an airplane rise off the ground. An airplane's wings are designed to create lift when the plane is moving. Lift happens when air moves faster on top of a wing than below it. This air movement takes pressure off the top of a wing. Lift lets the airplane rise.

WEIGHT AND DRAG

Weight is the force of **gravity**. Gravity pulls objects down to Earth. An airplane has to fight weight, or gravity, to stay in the air. Weight would make an airplane fall toward Earth if the engine did not produce enough thrust to keep it moving forward.

Drag also works against the airplane. Drag is the force of **friction**. Friction slows objects down when they move against each other. Wind is a type of drag because it slows down the plane as it moves over the aircraft.

The forces of flight help make even the simplest airplanes fly.

thrust—the force that pushes a vehicle forward
lift—the upward force of air that causes an object to fly
drag—the force that resists the motion of an object moving through the air
gravity—a force that pulls objects with mass together; gravity pulls objects down toward the center of Earth
friction—a force created when two objects rub together; friction slows down objects

THE FOUR FORCES OF FLIGHT

The Wright brothers could build and fly an airplane because they understood the four forces of flight needed to make an airplane fly.

Drag slows down the airplane. As the plane moves through the air, the forward motion of the plane is met with resistance from the wind. This is a form of drag.

Lift helps the airplane rise. When air moves faster on top of a wing than below it, the pressure below the wing is stronger, which lifts up the plane. The lift must be strong enough to overcome the plane's weight.

LIFT

ENGINE

THRUST

Thrust is the force that moves the airplane forward. The airplane's engine creates thrust. The plane's thrust must be stronger than the drag.

WEIGHT

Weight is the force of gravity, which pushes the airplane back toward the ground.

5

THE WORLD BEGINS TO FLY

Airplanes changed the world. It didn't take long before many countries realized that airplanes could be useful. In 1908 the Wright brothers began making planes for the U.S. Army. Airplanes were first used as weapons during World War I (1914–1918). Then during World War II (1939–1945), airplanes were one of the main weapons used in battle.

World War I was the first war in which airplanes were widely used.

WARPLANES

At first, warplane pilots simply flew over enemy territory to spy on them. The pilots wanted to get information on the enemy's location and number of troops and weapons. They used this information to prepare the ground troops for battle. Next, warplanes added machine guns and fierce fighting took place in the skies. Later, a special hatch was added to warplanes so they could drop bombs over enemy territory. It wasn't until World War II that planes were used to transport troops.

The airplane also changed travel and business. The first passenger airplane began service in Florida in 1914. The plane took off and landed on water and carried one passenger at a time. For $5 (about $125 today), a person could cross Tampa Bay in about 20 minutes. A boat needed 2 hours to make the same trip. A train needed 4 to 12 hours because it had to go all the way around the water. Going by automobile took 20 hours at the time.

Passengers board an airplane in the 1920s.

CHARLES LINDBERGH

In the early 1900s, many people were afraid to travel by airplane. They thought planes were unsafe.

But Charles Lindbergh changed the way people felt about flying. In 1927 he flew from New York City to Paris, France. He was the first person to fly alone across the Atlantic Ocean. His flight made people excited about air travel. After his flight, more businesses started building airplanes to carry passengers.

Lindbergh's flight took 33.5 hours. He flew without stopping for 3,600 miles (5,794 km).

NEW LAWS

Laws were introduced to make airplanes safer for travelers. In the United States the Air Commerce Act of 1926 made many rules for air travel. Planes had to be tested for safety, and pilots had to pass tests before they could be allowed to fly.

In 1967 the Federal Aviation Administration (FAA) was formed. The FAA sets rules to help make air travel safe. If a plane crashes, it is the FAA's job to find out why.

Charles Lindbergh stands next to his airplane, the *Spirit of St. Louis*. In 1927 Lindbergh flew his plane across the Atlantic Ocean.

6 AIRPLANES TODAY

After the Wright brothers, inventors began making airplanes larger and faster. They also added controls to make planes safer. These instruments help pilots fly at night or in unsafe weather. Radar and **air traffic control** also make flying safer.

Today's airplanes have lots of safety controls.

PASSENGER AIRPLANES

The first modern passenger airplane was the Boeing 247, which was introduced in 1933. The Boeing 247 traveled at a speed of 189 miles (304 km) per hour and carried just 10 passengers.

In 1976 the Concorde became the first airplane to make **supersonic** passenger flights. It could fly more than 1,300 miles (2,092 km) per hour. In fact, it only took 3.5 hours to fly from London to New York City. Even today it takes other planes eight hours to make the same trip. However, only the very rich could afford to fly on the Concorde. By 2003, when the Concorde made its last flight, a one-way ticket from London to New York City cost more than $6,000.

DID YOU KNOW?

Because the Concorde traveled so fast, it took more fuel to fly it. On average, the Concorde used about 6,770 gallons (25,627 liters) of fuel per hour. That's four times as much as a regular airplane.

air traffic control—ground staff who monitor and direct airplanes in flight and before and after takeoff
supersonic—faster than the speed of sound (767 miles/1,234 km per hour)

Most of today's passenger airplanes fly 460–575 miles (740–925 km) per hour. But engineers continue to build faster airplanes. There are currently plans to build other supersonic planes, similar to the Concorde, but with much more affordable ticket prices.

The F-15 Eagle is one of the most successful U.S. military planes in combat history. It has a top speed of 1,875 miles (3,018 km) per hour.

DID YOU KNOW?

Today, the largest passenger airplane is the Airbus A380. It has two floors and can carry up to 615 passengers.

Some military planes can fly more than 1,800 miles (2,897 km) per hour. In 2004 NASA set a world record with a **scramjet engine**-powered aircraft that reached nearly 7,000 miles (11,265 km) per hour! That's almost 10 times faster than the speed of sound!

Over time, planes became a more common way to travel. Now there are more than 100,000 flights all over the world every day. These flights carry hundreds of millions of passengers to their destinations.

Traveling by airplane has also become much safer. Pilots train for years before they can fly an airplane. Plus, two pilots are required to fly passenger planes—a captain and a copilot. If something happens to the captain during a flight, the copilot can step in and land the airplane safely.

INTO SPACE

The airplanes of the future could be faster and hold more passengers. They could even travel to space! The Virgin Galactic company is testing a passenger plane called WhiteKnightTwo that could be fast and powerful enough to one day take passengers to space and back.

scramjet engine—a type of engine in which combustion takes place in supersonic airflow

NOTABLE AIRPLANES SINCE 1914

THE ST. PETERSBURG-TAMPA AIRBOAT LINE
1914
1 pilot, 1 passenger
64 miles (103 km) per hour

SPIRIT OF ST. LOUIS
1927
1 pilot
120 miles (193 km) per hour

BOEING 247
1933
2 pilots, 10 passengers
189 miles (304 km) per hour

CONCORDE
1976
2 pilots, 100 passengers
1,354 miles (2,179 km) per hour

AIRBUS A380
2005
2 pilots, 544–615 passengers
587 miles (945 km) per hour

TIMELINE

1480s	Leonardo da Vinci draws designs for his ornithopter
1783	The Montgolfier brothers test the first hot-air balloon
1804	Sir George Cayley builds a special model glider that looks somewhat like a modern airplane
1853	Cayley creates the first full-scale glider that makes a successful flight with a passenger
1891	Otto Lilienthal makes his first hang glider and becomes the first person to make repeated successful flights
1903	Wilbur and Orville Wright build and launch the *Flyer,* the world's first successful airplane
1914	The first aircraft passenger service begins in Florida
1914–1918	Many new military airplanes are created for use in World War I
1927	Charles Lindbergh becomes the first person to fly alone across the Atlantic Ocean
1933	The Boeing 247 becomes the first modern passenger plane
1976	The Concorde becomes the first passenger plane to fly supersonic (faster than the speed of sound)
2003	The Concorde is retired because of low passenger numbers
2005	The Airbus A380, the world's largest passenger plane, makes its first passenger flight

GLOSSARY

aircraft (AIR-kraft)—a vehicle that flies through the air

air traffic control (AIR TRAF-ik kuhn-TROHL)—ground staff who monitor and direct airplanes in flight and before and after takeoff

aviation (ay-ve-AY-shuhn)—the science of building and flying aircraft

design (di-ZYN)—to create the shape or style of something

destination (des-tuh-NAY-shuhn)—the place where someone is traveling

drag (DRAG)—the force that resists the motion of an object moving through the air

engineer (en-juh-NEER)—someone trained to design and build machines, vehicles, bridges, roads, or other structures

friction (FRIK-shuhn)—a force created when two objects rub together; friction slows down objects

glider (GLYE-dur)—a lightweight aircraft that flies by floating and rising on air currents instead of by engine power

gravity (GRAV-uh-tee)—a force that pulls objects with mass together; gravity pulls objects down toward the center of Earth

lift (LIFT)—the upward force of air that causes an object to fly

mechanics (muh–KAN–iks)—a part of science that deals with the way forces affect still or moving objects

propeller (pruh-PEL-ur)—a rotating blade that provides the force to move an aircraft through the air

scramjet engine (SKRAM-jet EN-juhn)—a type of engine in which combustion takes place in supersonic airflow

supersonic (soo-pur-SON-ik)—faster than the speed of sound (767 miles/1,234 km per hour)

thrust (THRUHST)—the force that pushes a vehicle forward

CRITICAL THINKING QUESTIONS

1. Until the late 1800s, most people did not travel very far from their homes. Travel was often slow and uncomfortable. In what ways have airplanes made travel better today?

2. Choose two airplanes from the book, one early and one modern. Using the text and photos, compare and contrast the two airplanes. How has the modern plane changed from the early one?

3. Imagine you are one of the first passengers on Virgin Galactic's WhiteKnightTwo aircraft into space. Describe your experience on board the historic flight.

READ MORE

Grove, Tim. *Milestones of Flight: From Hot-Air Balloons to SpaceShipOne*. New York: Abrams Books for Young Readers, 2016.

Spilsbury, Louise. *The Wright Brothers and the Airplane*. Inventions that Changed the World. PowerKids Press, 2016.

White, Rowland. *Cleared for Takeoff: The Ultimate Book of Flight*. San Francisco: Chronicle Books, 2016.

INTERNET SITES

Use FactHound to find Internet sites related to this book.

Visit www.facthound.com

Just type in 9781515798415 and go.

INDEX

Air Commerce Act 23
Airbus A380 26, 28, 29
airplanes
  Concorde 25, 26, 28, 29
  Flyer 14–15, 29
  Spirit of St. Louis 23, 28
  WhiteKnightTwo 27
airscrew 10
automobile 7, 8, 9, 10, 21

Cayley, Sir George 12, 29

da Vinci, Leonardo 10, 29
drag 16, 17, 18, 19

Federal Aviation Administration (FAA) 23
forces of flight 16–19
friction 17

glider 12, 13, 14, 29
Great Chatsworth Train Wreck 9

helicopter 4–5, 10
horse and wagon 6, 7
hot-air balloon 11, 29

lift 16, 19
Lilienthal, Otto 13, 29
Lindbergh, Charles 22, 23, 29

military planes 20, 26, 27, 29
  F-15 Eagle 26
Montgolfier, Jacques-Étienne 11, 29
Montgolfier, Joseph-Michel 11, 29

NASA 27

ornithopter 10, 29

passenger planes 21, 25–27, 29

radar 24

scramjet engine 27
supersonic flight 25, 26, 29

thrust 16, 17, 19
train 7, 8, 9, 10, 21

Virgin Galactic 27

weight 16, 17, 19
World War I 20, 29
World War II 20
Wright, Milton 4–5
Wright, Orville 4–5, 14–15, 18, 20, 24, 29
Wright, Wilbur 4–5, 14–15, 18, 20, 24, 29